Dreg City

Matt Ross

Dreg City
Copyright © 2013 by Matthew Ross

All rights reserved. No part of this book may be reproduced or transmitted in any form or by any means without written permission from the author.

ISBN – 13:978-1489548184

Printed by Dead Sparrow Press

Dedicated to the Offended

you life is you fault

oct/26/19

Table of Contents

Introduction 7
The Bowels of Dreg City **8**
A Streetcar Named Balls 9
The Job 10
Bored 12
Bathroom Stalls of Broker Dreams 13
The Ladies of Houston's 15
Nadia, I think 17
My own little piece of Somalia 18
Fakebook 20
My View 22
Love poem to my couch 23
Roncies 24
The Man with the Pot 25
Amateur Comedy Night at "Not My Dog" 26
On the Streetcar again in Dreg City 30
My Hangover is Talkative 31
Work 33
the night my soul died again 36
Cockroaches 38
Chinatown Blues 39
The Mindset of a Dreg **41**
Reality of the Multitude 42
Material Heroin 43
hypocrisy of the sheeple 44
firearms? 45

War with Humanity 46
a lie is much prettier than the truth 47
Shit 49
The Leper Prince 50
The Bleakness 52
There's energy in the line 53
The Eyes See Lies as Truth 55
from the inside looking in 56
Wild Freedom 57
Whole Halves 59
the anger I feel inside 60
beauty in life 61
Inevitable 62
god? 64
The Smartest Man in the World 65
Sane Lunatics 66
Modern Day Bukowski 67
Space Invaders 68
Little Miracles (for Slayden) 69
The Breath of Chance 70
Don't Look in the Mirror 71
There's Drama in the Spiders Approach 72
Sanely, Insane 73
The Most Beautiful Angel of All 74
If 76
The Order of Chaos 77
Good, Evil or Will 78
Time? 80
We all die at the end 82
Montreal (somebody's Dreg City but not mine) 83
Montreal 84

Hotel Le Cantlie I apologize but I'm not sorry 86

All Hail the King 88

Alice 91

Jewish Jersey Girl in Montreal 96

Acknowledgements 98

Contact Information 99

Introduction

This book of poetry is born out of big city living. It's an all out attack on conformity and a swift kick to the nuts for people who think they're individuals but really aren't. It explores the unfortunate reality of working 40 hours a week, daily commutes, public transit, bums, bars, women, the half dead people you face everyday and some of my personal philosophies on life in general.

The first section of the book called "The Bowels of Dreg City" deals with the day to day experiences of living in an empty, materialistic society whose reality is based on news, sitcoms, magazines, fashion, politics and shopping.

The second section entitled "The Mindset of a Dreg" is an examination of the hypocrisy of mankind in general. From the smiley faced politicians to the fakeness of most people you encounter in this world. It's a love note to the ignorant and the offended.

The third section "from the inside looking in" focuses on life, death, time, space, god, science and my interpretation of them.

The last section is a series of poems that outline a trip I took with 5 friends to Montreal for St. Patty's day weekend.

This book will entertain, disgust, educate, and challenge your views on many things. My ask is for you to keep an open mind and continue on because you just might find some insight into the society you're a part of and the life you live. If you find a poem you like be sure to read it out loud so you can experience it to its fullest.

The King of the Dregs,

Matt Ross

The Bowels of Dreg City

A Streetcar Named Balls

I sat in a single seat
Beside the doors in the middle of the streetcar
Finally a roomy seat to call my own
Slowly the dregs of society pack in
Like a constipated streetcar
Still, I'm okay
My seat is roomy
Then this big black man in a jester hat parks
himself right in front of me
His balls eye level
5 inches from my face and they stink
I cringe on the inside
Does this man get some twisted pleasure out of
flaunting around his stinky nuts?
The odor of 10 day old underwear attacks me
An apocalyptic blend of stale urine, shit and old sweat
This must be what real poverty smells like
Regardless
Why me?
I finally get a good seat and this is what happens
Ya maybe I should have given my seat to that 80
year old lady with the crutches
but still
why can't I get a hot girl
in tight pants
waving her ass in my face?
A street car stripper
Hell even a nice smelling homosexual would have
been preferable to this bastard
But no
not me
I get the man with the stinky nuts
Fuck I hate street cars

The Job

Alone and down
Sitting on the couch
Thinking about the job
and the murder of my youth
Knowing why I put up with it
Money
The almighty dollar
The addiction no one can seem to shake
What if I quit?
What would my life become?
Would I still have friends?
Could I survive?
Pigeons survive without it
Why can't I?
What could I do instead?
Writing
Music
Poetry
How much does that pay?
uhhghhh
I don't know man
but I can't continue what I'm doing for much longer
Especially the little deaths you face everyday
The boss telling you that your tone of voice offended
some fucken coward you work with
The meetings about statistics and performance
Looking around the table and seeing people
who actually care about their shitty work world
Thinking about their lives is actually more depressing
then thinking about my own
at least I don't see my future in this place
The urinals covered in different colored pubes with perfect little puddles of piss right below them
Endless emails of nothingness
The only turn on is the hot chick in tight pants

Hoping for a periodic glimpse of her sweet ass
taking a picture with your mind for later
Some of the people are cool but
most are fucken dirtbags
Fuck the job
I need something else
Even if that means living with the cockroaches typing on
an old computer, drinking cheap beer, smoking
cheap cigarettes, broke and out of work
It's still preferable to the job
When life becomes a job
that's when it's time to quit
Don't be the job
Find another way
or die trying

Bored

Sitting at my desk bored
Recovering from last nights hangover
Cold sweat gross like a humid summer day
A shower would be nice but it's not possible
I look at the clock
3:14pm
Now it's 3:15pm
and I can't wait to get to fuck outta here
The fan blows on my arm to keep me fresh
Sometimes I move it to my face but
my eyes start to water
Conversations all around me
My employees talking to their clients
I guess my life could be worse
I could be doing that
Random mouse clicks
My belly rumbles
It feels like slow moving jelly creeping towards heaven's gate
My asshole in better words
I have to shit
It'll be my third of the day
My boss walks by
I minimize the poem
I hear him rustling paper
I think he's opening a chocolate bar
He makes a phone call and whispers
I'm interrupted by a person wanting to know something
I answer his question
The phone rings
I don't answer
It's 3:30pm
I'm still bored
I think I'll go for that shit

Bathroom Stalls of Broken Dreams

I love taking shits
but not at work
It's always such a process
You need to inspect each stall
and choose the least filthy
Oh Great there's piss all over the seat in stall one
I wonder to myself
Who did this and why?
What kind of degenerate fuck are you?
Probably some nobodies only way to get back at the world for treating him like the piece of shit he is
I'm sure he's hated by most
Loathed by the opposite sex
Can't get laid in real life and pissing all over the seat is the only dignity he has left
His very own vulgar display of power
Or maybe he's just a bad pisser
What's behind stall number two?
Survey says
A Shit Sundae
And the crowd applauds violently in my head
What kind of demented soul puts toilet paper in the bowl first
then takes a shit on top of it and leaves it floating there for everyone to see?
A fucken idiot, that's who
Anyways on to the third and final stall
Dear God please don't be a dead body in here
It doesn't look too bad
A couple of pubes on the seat
No big deal
I wipe'em off, sit down and push
I'm about to breathe a sigh of relief when the bathroom door opens
I hear all this crashing around
Somebody frantically opening and closing stall doors
Turning taps on and off

Toilets flushing
A mop comes under my door and starts washing my feet
A man mumbles under his breath "Sick Fucks"
I laugh a little and completely agree
Poor janitor
Poor me
I couldn't wait just another 5 minutes before coming into this
Horror,
oh the horror
Shitty timing as usual
What would life be without it?
We're all born between piss and shit anyways
Might as well enjoy it

The Ladies of Houston's

In their black or white dresses
Tight fitted beautiful young bodies
Little underwear stretched across their asses
Breasts bursting like clouds of flesh
Waiting for one of them to make an adjustment
Skin vibrant and painted
Talkative dancers of the night
Filipino Princess
Half Indian and German Goddess
With her black hair, brown eyes and salmon lips
Shoulders broad and proud
Who laughs with her whole body
DJ spinning tunes of our youth
Matty Runge bold and engaging
Telling the girls what he likes about them
Which is everything!
Geops roboting and screaming
      "Oh yeah boy"
His main goal is to take off his shirt
and get some ass
G sitting and watching the chaos ensue
Enjoying the rebirth
his new friends have given him
Mikey B
3 drinks deep
Ready to dance
All his feet need is time and space
His energy will do the rest
Everyone hollering and
laughing at the beautiful confusion
Pricey checking out the girls
but refusing to be introduced
A classy establishment
turned into a dirty basement jam
The other patrons join in

Buying drinks for the Dregs
they can't seem to take their eyes off of
The waitresses and hostesses
get off, change and join in
Each one sexy and unique in their own way
Wonderful creatures of the night
Making life worth it a few hours at a time
Uniting our spirits and moving as one
Inspiring this ode to them
The Ladies of Houston's

Nadia, I think

Leather clad
Ukrainian girl
Tall dark hair
Eyes like brown fire
Poet
Jameson drinking
Beautiful piece of flesh
Kissing wet rain
Read my poem
and laughed
like she should
girl of my nightmare's dream
lover of my broken heart
on display
in my world of words
and physical experience
life bleeds thunder
lightning flashes blood red
night temptress
Parkdale resident
I wait for your text
with anticipation and
bated breath
so we can write
life together
for at least
a little while

My own little piece of Somalia

I met up with one of my ex-girlfriends the other day
We hit a bar called "Wide Open"
$2.50 drink Thursdays from 5-8
She looks sexy in her business girl suit
Perfect ass and tits
I think back to when I had them
and they were nice
We start talking and drinking
I'm reminded of why I liked her
She's funny and digs the same kinds of bars I do
prefers a more working class feel
doesn't really care for the corporate culture
I understand
I'm the same way
She's tall
looks like David Bowie's wife Iman
With her lips
her soft, soft lips
My own little piece of Somalia
She orders a double rum and coke
Now I know the party's on
The bar is packed
Tunes pumpin
People watchin
The clock ticks
and it's already time for her to leave
She has responsibilities now
We barrel our way through the crowd
Her in front of me
I start grabbing her ass
Rubbing my piece up against it
She playfully slaps my hands away
and accidentally slaps my joint
I get semi
We reach outside and start smoking

She comes up close and looks me in the eye
I try to kiss her
but she turns away
We start walking down the street
I pull her in close
Arm and arm
We stop and I kiss her
No tongue just lips
I suck on her bottom lip
Glad to know at least one other place its been
I grab her ass for old time's sake
She laughs
I wave her down a cab
and she leaves
What a magnificent woman
I say to myself

Fakebook

I like things
Sometimes pictures of peoples families
Sometimes a cute picture of a dog or someone else's dinner
Sometimes I like baby pictures
or new pictures of old friends
or pictures of nice cars
or stupid thoughts
What do people think when they see my name?
Maybe I was some girl's first kiss
Maybe I was your class President
Maybe you saw me play a show
Maybe you've known me since we were kids and think about all those times we walked to 7-11 together
Never knowing what was gonna happen or who we were gonna meet
The neighbourhood was our Facebook
Our bikes were our cell phones
Our lives unmonitored and free
We went for coffee and smoked cigarettes
We stole booze from our parents and drank it in baseball field's
We lit fires and shoplifted from gas stations
We were rebels in our own minds
We talked about girls and hoped to bump into them
We climbed Snow Mountains in parking lots and threw each other off of them
We jumped on other peoples trampolines
We got in fights with kids from other schools
We fought each other
We thought being a Mallrat was cool
We would listen to the radio with a blank tape, wait for a song we liked and record it
We never worried about the rent or mortgages or kids or careers or how the world actually functioned
We got to know each other through our conversations and the actions we took
People used to think the eyes were the window to the soul

Now it seems Facebook is
People reduced to random pictures and comments
Lives reduced to entries on a computer
Letters on a screen
Ones and zeros
To a false representation of what they want you to think their lives have become
To a fakebook of reference
Or maybe it is a true portrayal of their lives
In which case is even sadder
It seems to me the majority of people are living the same kinds of lives
Huxley would be proud
Same with Orwell
Not of what society has or will become
but because they were right!

My View

Sitting here
watching my view
at Roncesvalles and Queen
high up on Triller Ave
The sun strangles me with its beauty
Like an A-bomb
frozen at its Zenith
Red like the devils heart
I look at the lake
dark blue
swallowed up
by the greed of man
You have to call
a toll free number
before swimming
to ensure it's safe
Not even Jesus
would eat the fish from here
The highway snakes around
the lake like a bent right elbow
Cars coming and going
from the bowels of Dreg City
Like flashing white blood cells
fighting off the disease of nature
the sky burns
periwinkle orange
as the machine
is fed
the life and times
of everyone in it

Love poem to my couch

I love my couch
I could lay on you all day
every day
for the rest of my life
I sleep on you
have sex on you
even with other people
you hug me with comfort
I play my guitar and sing to you
Write songs with you
I look out the window at the view from you
I watch the moon 3 times a month with you
I eat most of my meals with you
I think, drink and dream on you
I smoke cigarettes and try not to burn you
blow joints with you
have conversations with my friends on you
write poems on you
talk on the phone with you
I spend most of my free time with you
and you don't ask for anything in return
you are selfless
you don't talk back to me
you let me fart and don't complain about it
you don't mind if I'm naked or clothed
you don't judge me
you don't care if I'm stinky or sweaty
you don't mind if I swear
you accept me for me
you let me use you whenever I want
and no matter what you're always there to comfort me
my beautiful couch
my angelic couch
how I love you

Roncies

The heaven of Parkdale
Little Poland
Mom and Pop shops
Restaurants, bookstores, café's, bars, grocers
Walking up the street is an adventure in itself
People and their dogs
Big dogs
Little dogs
Yappy dogs
Pooping dogs
Peeing dogs
Dogs on leashes
Dogs off leashes
Every kind of dog you can imagine
Families pushing strollers
Little kids on scooters
Homeless guy in wheelchair drinking Listerine
Beggin for change
Musicians playing guitar or violin or saxophone
Beggin for change
Hipsters hideout
Me walking
Beggin for space
The last standing community in Dreg City
The one place I feel anonymous
The Pride of Parkdale
A secret that must be kept from the 905
I sit on a little patio
order a Tyskie
and watch the people walk by

The Man with the Pot

Walking up Harvard Street
to Triller
I see a man holding a big pot
Almost coddling it
He stops to talk to himself
I get a little closer
The pot has a thick yellow sludge in it
The guy screams
    GET AWAY FROM ME!
I ignore him
He starts puking into the pot
That same yellow gunk
Arm around it
Protecting it
Not unlike Gollum and the ring
I keep walking
Undisturbed
I look across the street
and see a father teaching his son
how to shoot a basketball
Such strange polarities
Ah well
Just another
ordinary day
in Parkdale

Amateur Comedy Night at "Not My Dog"

I walk in late and drunk to mild applause
Not for me but somebody else
It's Amateur Comedy Night at
Parkdale bar, Not My Dog
I order a Moosehead and take in the crowd
Some MC comes up to the mic
He notices there's very little energy in the room
Probably cuz a' all those terrible comics that came on before my arrival
He introduces the next comedian
Bill Shulakistica or some shit like that
He doesn't use the mic but
instead has a podium
He starts his routine with a
political rant only he understands
The energy that was left in the room filters out like the air of a balloon
He pulls out a top hat and says
  "Can anyone here guess what I'm gonna do with this?"
  -Take a shit in it- I say
A couple people snicker
He pauses slightly in shock,
  "Nnnooo, I'm gonna take these 2 balls out and juggle them"
The crowd laughs cuz that's almost as ridiculous as him taking a shit in it
He starts juggling and the crowd waits
He finishes to sparse applause
Kinda like a parent clapping for
someone else's kid at a recital
The true sound of apathy
The MC looking depressed
introduces the next comic
  "This is Candace something or other and she's deaf"
I start laughing cuz I think it's a joke

Then up comes this sexy little thing in tight jeans, blonde hair and a fuck you attitude
Just how I like'em
She starts talking
> "Hoz eveybudy doin tonit"
> you know, like how deaf people talk

I'm thinking
Damn this hot piece of ass really is deaf
She kicks off her set with a few jokes
Then she starts talking about how guys stereotype deaf girls
> "They tink I'l fuk d'em on de first date cuz I'ne deaf"

The crowd starts laughing
> "They tink I'l jump on dem and buk dem like a bronco"
> -That's what I thought- I say

The crowd damn near erupts in laughter
but stop themselves as
if suddenly realizing the political incorrectness of heckling a deaf girl
Not me
I don't care if you're a
one legged midget with a hair lip
I'll still heckle you
Don't get on the stage if you can't take it
I thought she was good though
The deaf girl finishes her set and the MC comes back to introduce the next comedian
A guy approaches me and asks me for a cigarette
I give him one and he asks me to join him
We go down and up the stairs to the back patio
We light up and he starts talking

> "Hey man, what's with the heckling? We do this comedy night every Thursday and just so you're aware everybody in that room upstairs knows each other. You're the only person nobody knows. I don't think you realize how close you are to getting your ass kicked. I mean it's one thing to heckle a comedian but a deaf girl, don't get me wrong it was funny as hell but I strongly recommend you stop the heckling."

-Alright man thanks for letting me know-

We go back inside the bar
I look around at the crowd and
notice their all giving me dirty looks
They're glaring at me like
they just smelt shit or something
like some sort of villain
And it feels good
These motherfuckers don't want a heckler
Fuck'em
Don't go in the forest if
you're afraid of the wolves
The next comedian starts his set
    "Did you hear about the girl with two vaginas?"
    -You shouldn't talk about your mother that way- I scream
A couple people start laughing and holding on to their guts for dear life
the others chuckle under their breath
as if they're hiding something
Even the comedian can't help himself
Eventually they start taking shots at me
    "What you think about that ya long haired fuck"
The crowd explodes with laughter
They're all thinking the same thing
Finally somebody is going after
that piece of shit heckler
The crowd starts getting more
and more into the show
Laugh harder and harder
They even start laughing at my heckles
In fact they look forward to them
By the end of the show
everyone's drinking and hugging each other
Even me
A guy comes up and puts his arm around me
    "Hey man you're a pretty funny guy"

The bartender sends me over a free beer
I felt like Rocky when he fought
Ivan Drago in Russia
Hated at first and loved at the end
It's a fine line between a heel and a hero
Those who stick to being themselves will
feel the power of both and
prevail in the end
Don't ever stop being you
Even if that means
being the most despised person in the crowd
They'll always notice you
but they're fickle
Sometimes they're with you
Sometimes they're against you
Sometimes in the same night
It's nothing personal
They don't know any better
Remember that

On the Streetcar again in Dreg City

On the Streetcar again in Dreg City
looking out the window
at Trinity Bellwoods park
Heading East on Queen Street
I see a girl jogging
her pony tail
bobbing up and down
her cheeks rosie
spandex tight pants
I wonder what she looks like
in regular clothes
how she talks
what she's into
I wonder what she feels like
I wonder what she looks like naked
The guy sitting beside me belches
little projectiles
fly out of his mouth like escaped convicts
My daydream ruined
I sit back
and wait
for my next little
death

My Hangover is Talkative

I woke up this morning
with a perfect headache
a thirst that needed quenching
and a stomach in need of evacuating
My hangover sits on my skull
like a Facehugger alien
My whole body can feel It start talking to me
    "Great night, last night hey Matt"
    -I've had better-
    "How do you plan on getting to work?"
    -You know how, I'm taking the Streetcar-
    "Please don't, I'll puke"
My hangover begins to sweat
You know, that cold dirty sweat
you get on humid days in polluted cities
I agree with my hangover
I don't wanna to take the streetcar either
But that's how it is in Dreg City
Watching the vacant parking lot
lives of other people pass by
where buying a new car
is their greatest aspiration
The kind of people
who've never had a conversation with themselves
let alone their hangovers
Speaking of which
I'm interrupted rudely by My hangover
The son of a bitch is attacking me
It feels like he's pounding my insides
with a rubber hammer
My ribs hurt
My muscles are sweating
My soul is dehydrated
And I don't have time for a shower
I dress and look in the mirror

Not bad

I put some eye drops in and I head out the door

My hangover begins talking again

    "Matt please don't take the streetcar

    I'll get sick"

    -What if I get a seat by the window

    open it so the cold air can blow on My face thus preventing You from puking?-

    "I'm alright with that"

I get on the streetcar

get the window seat as planned

open it

and my hangover breathes a sigh of relief

    "ahhhhh"

As usual the street car fills up

Some lady sits behind me and the first thing she says (in a Rosie Perez type voice)

    "Excuse me sir could you close your window, it's cold in here"

My hangover cringes and I say

    -Listen lady, the only thing stopping me from puking right now is the cold air blowing on my face, I have a hangover with its own personality that won't survive this trip without it. This window is Jesus Christ to my hangover-

The lady says nothing and moves

I get through the rest of the ride

with no further problems

Except the fact

I have to work for another 8 hours

None the less my hangover is pleased

He gets the rest of the day off while I work

That's alright with me though

Cuz I couldn't get through

this job without him

Thanks little buddy

You're a life saver

Work

Waste my time
5 days a week
8 hours a day
Plus the commute
People on the subway
Barely alive
Coughing
Standing
Waiting their opportunity to steal the next available seat
Cripples, old people and pregnant ladies be damned
Comfort trumps all
Open mouth breathers
Pretenders
Working to pay their mortgages
credit cards
car loans
overdraft
personal lines of credits
next vacation to an all in resort one week at a time
Think they're alive because of all the things they have but don't own
Wondering what's gonna happen on next weeks episode of the Bachelor
Reading up on the latest gossip in their commuter magazines
Don't know who Charles Bukowski is or why he matters
Listening to their Iphones, Ipads, Iwatches, Blackberry's, MP3 players or whatever god damn hip device they can get their sticky little fingers on
Filling themselves with emptiness
Letting their eyes become voids of colour
Watching their children slip into the abyss
Thinking it's a mountain of opportunity
Watching the clock tick never realizing time doesn't matter
until it runs out
In need of direction
only to consult Google

Mapquest
Wikipedia
Imdb
Amazon
Ebay
Facebook
Just as long as it's not human
Trusting in the freedom of the internet
The storage unit of human information
The new subconscious
Artificial brain of forever
Not capable of feeling
Just able to suggest
Slowly the information will be manipulated
All physical books
cd's
records
and movies will be deemed obsolete
and destroyed
Events like September 11th will be rewritten
again
Those in power will be able to erase anyone's life with the push of a button
Martin Luther who
John Lemon
Kurt Dobain
Jeepus Cripes
Allen Einsted
Adolf Hitler will be a god
So will George W. Bush
and Obama
and Stephen Harper
The new religion will be technology
Made to control
track
monitor
record

and predict
Until you won't even be able to take a shit without being watched
And those same people on the subway
won't care
They'll go to their nine to five's
Listen to their music
Thinking their lives are better than most
and I'll go on writing
living
and hating the machine

the night my soul died again

Alone again
wind whistling
through the door of my apartment
smoking a cigarette
playing guitar
watching TV
listening to the neighbours go to war with each other
looking out my window at the pigeons flying
one of them lands on my balcony
I'm amazed at how easily they can do this
it coo's a bit
turns its head around
looks right at me
and takes a big white shit
angered I get up and
chase the cocky bastard away
I think about masturbation
pull my phone out to search for some porn
I change my mind
I consider cleaning my apartment
I just can't bring myself to do it
lost in my thoughts
thinking about it all
concluding
that nothing kills the soul more
than the mundane little things
from cleaning the apartment
to clippin nails
to doing laundry
to getting on a packed streetcar
just so you can make someone else shit loads of money
to line ups for coffee
to random loud noises
to the sun blasting you in the eyes
when you're already hungover

to idiotic conversations around you about fitness routines
to gay guys that sound like gay guys
to dreams more obnoxious then appearances
to bums and anybody who wants something for nothing
to ugly people who think their pretty
to pretty people who think their ugly
It's the insignificant things that kill your soul
over and over and over again

Cockroaches

I have a lot in common with cockroaches
They're forced to adapt to humanity
So am I
They don't like the light
Hide in dark places, scare and creep people out
Are hated on sight
Survive in spite all efforts to destroy them
Are hunted by most
Loved by one
Themselves
How do they not have their own civilization yet?
Had you been asked by evolution who will survive
The Human
The Dinosaur
or the Cockroach
What would you say?
You'd been wrong if you said Dinosaur
And humanity won't survive long enough to be proven
right about the ladder

Chinatown Blues

Broke down on the sidewalk
Chinatown
LCBO
Spadina and Dundas
Pregnant lady
Sitting in the crane position
drunk, drugged and passed out
with a jail house tattoo
of a scorpion and a cross on her chest
Surrounded by the lost
and hopeless
with some soul left
albeit grimey
Their motto
"Hey got some change"
Lined up against the wall like broken molested toys nobody wants to play with
The passers by walk just far enough to express on their face
what they feel in their gut
utter disgust
They'd rather watch 2 ladies and a cup
then deal with these dreg's
They actually feel sorry for themselves for having to experience such worthless human beings
Never considering their rage
sadness
desperation
child hoods
family lives
mental disorders
lack of nutrition
support
self esteem
or what it's like to be dangling
off the edge of a cliff

holding onto a hundred pound bag of your own shit
hoping for one of these passers by to pull you up
from the hole you're in
only to see them sneer
ignore
judge and curse your very existence
Silently hoping for you to let go
not of the shit but of the edge
One less bum in Dreg City
The only people in your life are damaged flesh mannequins
looking for any fix
drugs
alcohol
mouth wash
turpentine
Anything that can help them forget reality
the horror of everyday life
the starvation of wasted decisions
the self loathing
future fearing
present blurring
past hating
tragedies of humanity
Stumble on…………

The Mindset of a Dreg

Reality of the Multitude

Fakeness grows in humans like leaves on trees
Dangling off each branch of their existence
and slowly wilting away with the seasons
From the clothes they wear
to the magazines they read
It's there
Like a false sense of security
Something to discuss with the other lemmings
Mundane conversations are the best they can hope for
Claiming to be cultured
because they've been to a wine and cheese party
The rest of us bombarded
with their eerily similar fronts
And they spread faster then any known disease
To be expected when the bulk of their information comes from TV
Ground zero
The greatest polluter of minds since radio
Propaganda disguised
as sitcoms, dramas, advertising and news
Soon enough the internet will take its place
then the micro chip
or some sexy electronic device
with a hidden agenda
The harder they look the less they see
It's the eyes that lie
when the intellect is kept blind
The greatest of ironies is individually
humans can not agree to disagree
but collectively they'll tear flesh from bone
There's a glitch and the system's exploiting it
What can be done when an entire society needs an intervention?
Today the glass is half empty
Tomorrow, who knows?

Material Heroin

All most people want is a quick fix
Something to chase the dragon with
Veneers for their teeth
Implants for their breasts
A nose the masses will find appealing
Hair extensions
Rogaine for men
The penis pump
A never ending bottle of booze
A winning lottery ticket
Fame so they can get laid
Drugs to prepare them for the 9 to 5
Television to raise their children with
Education without teaching or having to do
Fast food restaurants
The strap
The knife
The gun
The bomb
The war machine
The world in not a problem they need to fix
Only their appearances
Their identities
Their clothes
Their veins
Their houses
Their cars
Their control over other peoples perception of themselves
Nothing else matters
Only the physical
Material heroin

hypocrisy of the sheeple

Another shooting in America
26 dead
20 of them children
Horrendous crime, no doubt
Those who watch TV weep
Update their Facebook statuses with condolences
and condemnations
Those in power push for stricter gun laws
because stricter gun laws will reduce the amount of psychotic mad men going on kill crazy rampages
While the bombs drop on Afghanistan
and soon Syria
30,000 dead civilians
Men, women and children
No mention of it in the western press
No tears shed by the public
No outrage
No calls for stricter "Bomb" or "War" laws
Operation Enduring Freedom Marches On
While the Sheeple
wait in line
for their next Christmas purchase

firearms?

11,493 firearm murders a year in the USA

16,799 by other means

25,500 dead from drug abuse

34,485 people die in car accidents

107,400 alcohol related deaths

378,000 casualties of war world wide per year

529,000 dead from tobacco in the USA alone

13,000,000 die from starvation every year

296,000,000 people murdered by Governments in the last 100 years

Now what should we ban?

War with Humanity

If I was a chicken
    I'd be at war with humanity
If I was a cow
    I'd be at war with humanity
I was the ocean or the air
    I'd be at war with humanity
If I was the plants and tree's
    I'd be at war with humanity
If I was a bus boy
    I'd be at war with humanity
If I was a banker
    I'd be at war with humanity
If I was a cashier working at a fast food restaurant
    I'd be at war with humanity
If I was a Rock Star
    I'd be at war with humanity
If I was a Poet
    I'd be at war with humanity
If I was a homeless guy, hooker or junkie
    I'd be at war with humanity
If I was a rat, cockroach or house millipede
    I'd be at war with humanity
If I was the CEO, President, Prime Minister, King, Queen, Pope or Ayatollah, I'd be just fine
cuz I'd already be at war with humanity
If I was an atheist, religious person or scientist
    I'd be at war with humanity
If I was the earth, universe and all existence
    I'd be at war with humanity
If I was God
    I'd be at war with humanity
If I was none of these things
    I'd be at war with humanity
What about you?

a lie is much prettier than the truth

Just ask the media
The Government
Religious Cults
Lawyers
Holy Men
Psychics
Politicians
Police officers
Corporations
Husbands
Wives
Girlfriends
Boyfriends
Mothers
Fathers
Daughters
Sons
Uncles
Aunts
Yourself
Experts
Any human capable of judging without thinking or proving
The Truth
Newspapers
Magazines
Santa Clause
Atheists
The Easter Bunny
The Tooth Fairy
Jesus Christ
Israel
The Prophet Muhammad
September 11th, 2001
The Reichstag fire of 1933
The Gulf of Tonkin

Fiat currency
Weapons of Mass destruction in IRAQ
The American Dream
Education
Trillion dollar bailouts
Democracy
which leads to bankruptcy
then Dictatorship
The diamonds of Africa
Slavery abolished by Lincoln
The meaning of mortgage
which is "death pledge"
The Federal Reserve
The Bank of Canada
Billions of poor and starving people dying in the streets
While the elite gorge
With their fuck you faces
Retractable eyes
Guillotine lips
Souls of tape worms
Hearts of jelly fish
Sociopathic killers
Glutton's of society
Vacuous black holes
Consumers of flesh
Power as virtue
Empathy as sin
Generation after generation
'Til the death of time

Shit

What's with this world, man?
With their Tetris champion
Donkey Kong **shit** eating wasted lives
who
If the bomb dropped
and civilization was teetering on
the edge of destruction
Wouldn't know **shit** if they had a mouth full of it
While an entire generation holds a college degree
and can't even get a job at McDonald's!
Am I the only one enraged by this?!!!!
Where the strong are emasculated for
their inherent aggression
unwillingness to conform and
overall instability
When a billion years of evolution doesn't mean **shit** unless you own
a TV station
Where you can say whatever you want and the people will find it cool
The blind leading the deaf in
a field of land minds
Listening and watching the new high priests of infotainment
    "Look that guy can **shit** standing up"
    "The economy's fine"
    "Nothing to worry here about folks"
    "The governments got your back"
Am I the only one that can see something's wrong here?
When a story about a biker doping is more important then your country at war
the theft of your personal liberty
and the murder of your children's future
There must be something wrong!
If you can't see the
lightning flash behind the mountain does the lightning exist?
I guess I'll have to ask the Wizard of Oz

The Leper Prince

It's a fine line between a leper and a prince
One minute you're on top of the world
Riding high on the bicycle of life
The crowds cheering on the 7 time champ
5 in a row
Unbeatable
Beautiful women seek you out
Kings, diplomats and the famous
wanna to be around you
wanna fuck you
Your drinks are free
Your food is free
Your soul is free
You think everything's free
Then you realize the price much too late
The press dig into you with their rusty hooks
They wanna find the dirt
Make it up if necessary
Allegations
Investigations
Lawyer's fees
The perfect man isn't so perfect
And the once cheering crowd now jeers
They laugh at you
Are enraged by you
Spit on you
Want blood from you
Feel betrayed by you
Sitting in their cubicles of judgment
They suck at your fall like an infant on its mother's tit
You go from the toast to the turd
Your famous friends won't even let you smell their shit
Let alone be seen in public with you
And the late show hosts will feast
Like hungry Piranha's

Not even your bones will remain
Then one day
they'll forget
at least for a little while
then they'll wanna come back
but this time you'll be stronger then ever
Meaner then ever
You'll be the villain
the one jeering
spitting
and laughing
Because you'll have come to the realization
that your life is a divine comedy
and a sincere tragedy
but you won't care
Cuz it was all worth it

The Bleakness

Everybody is a whore
Every man, woman, child, gutter bum & cripple
No one is free from it
We use our soul as a commodity
It is a hindrance for those without a god
Even more so for those with one
Who wants a conscience
in a conscienceless world?
Attack or be consumed
by the black hole
humanity has become
Our common strength
develops into our greatest weakness
Who needs morality when we have ambition?
Those who suffer are at fault for refusing to cure
the human disease of emotion
And those who care will be cast into the fire
As the flesh sizzles and pops
the multitudes will cheer
When madness becomes sanity
decency is merely a suggestion
Absurdity evolves into the new divinity
Our future built on the crushed skulls of the past
Do what thou wilt, will be the whole of the law
Mothers will kill daughters
Fathers will rape sons
Humans will eat humans
Blood, guts and tears will be the new delicacies
And feast they shall
Until once again the sane become insane
Lunacy as the remedy not the condition
It seems at times the madhouse is the safest place in the world to be
Leave the normal's to themselves
Their evolution will handle the rest

There's energy in the line

The villain is the hero
War is the answer
Living is dying
Freedom is slavery
The truth is my favorite lie
Rainbows are freaks of nature
The butterfly screams as the wolf stalks
Red is the colour of vengeance
The soul is made of flesh
so is god
There's no black without white
The world is a construct of words
My mind soars like the eagle over the fringe of civilization
Looking for its next meal
While the a-bomb drops
A dot in the sky
A product of thought
Caught in the machinery
Progress to oblivion
Can heaven smell napalm, burning skin and melted eyes?
Too bad the TV addicts can't feel the pain of the news they watch
If only eagles ate humans this planet might have a chance
Even the Devil has its limits
Humanity free to choose
Only to give up their rights to those
who "know better"
51 rules 49
The majority is always right
Has everyone forgotten about lynching?
The Dark Ages
Nazi, Germany
Communist Russia and China
Modern Day America
Often the leaders are blamed

Patsy's at best
What about the people?
They allow this to happen
Where's their blame?
Accomplices at the least
You charge a getaway driver with accessory to murder, even if they didn't pull the trigger, don't you?
The problem is not the leaders
It's the followers
It's always been the followers
Will always be the followers
Quit following

The Eyes See Lies as Truth

People have
been taught
that what
they see
with their eyes
not what
they see
with their hearts
is the truth
When people
start seeing
with their hearts
and not
their eyes
then and
only then
will mankind
have a chance

from the inside looking in

Wild Freedom

Too many people
spend too much of their time
worrying about death
and very little of their time
worrying about life
their hearts seem much older
then their eyes
and
their souls
mind
follows suit
Everyday they get a little closer to death
rather then a little closer to life
They're lives pass them by like cars in the rear view mirror
Thinking about the destination
not realizing
the journey
is the destination
and destiny
is always happening
Although
not in
a straight line
with a start and finish
Nobody really knows when they started
nor when they're finished
much like the big bang
we are a combination
of random events
bursting into life
out of the black nothingness
we all come from
and
return to
The point is

to go
and go and go
and go
like the last wild stallion
on the frontier of extinction
Watching its brothers and sisters
be rode on by proud humans
or pulling plows
or racing
or even being fucked by them
Humans are a demented species
Hell bent on domesticating everything
and nothing kills more than
domestication
An animal without freedom
is much like a human without it
boring as fuck
half dead
and waiting for its next order

Whole halves

My greatest strength is to find weakness in everything
My empathy is only matched by my disgust
My love only matched by my hate
My happiness only matched by my sadness
My madness only matched by my sanity
My evil only matched by my good
My wicked heart dreams of good deeds for selfish reasons
My soul screams for more flesh
but I'm lost in the physical world
covered in shadows
filled with spirits
on the edge of what is
and what is not
I dangle by a string off a mountain
staring into an ocean of mercy
embraced by the violence of nature
I ponder the condition of man
only to realize
it's the condition of animal
And we
the Fallen Angels
are set upon this earth
to feed
and feed
and feed and feed and feed and feed
and feed and feed and feed
and feed and feed
and feed

the anger I feel inside

The days burn and the sky
is scorched with the broken
promises of things I could have done
The hockey dream
a farce
Being a Conservation Officer
a joke
The bear eats meat
Living or dead
Do bears eat bear meat?
I'm ugly sure they do
So do humans
What's wrong with this god damn world?
Does everything eat everything?
It seems the species that doesn't
becomes food themselves
and eventually is swallowed by extinction itself
Eat or die,
that's reality

beauty in life

Most people see beauty in life
and so do I
but it's the ugliness in life that attracts me
the perfect shit
an angry homeless person
a leper with two fingers, three toes and the face of an elephant
a man on the streetcar screaming what sounds like military
orders in Chinese then hockin a lugee in his hand
the aftermath of the A-Bomb
the shock and awe of war
the fungus growth on the heel of my foot
belly button lint
vultures eating a rotting corpse
a very bad hang over
a good puke
the feeling you get when your chick cheats on you
the moment you realize you hate your life and take the nightmarish
steps required to change it
quitting the hundred thousand dollar a year job
giving up a comfy living in the lower upper echelon of Dreg City
from the boss to self employed
from rich corporate slave to poor freeman
I like the sound of that
a Poor Freeman
it seems to me most rich men started off as poor freemen
and so will I

Inevitable

Jesus died
Hitler died
Napoleon died
Manson lives
Stalin died
Mao died
Alexander the Great died
Gandhi died
Malcolm X died
Marx died
JFK died
Trudeau died
Lennon died
Cobain died
Ledger died
Bukowski died
Kerouac died
Jung died
Freud died
FDR died
Monroe Died
Bruce Lee died
Nebuchadnezzar died
Tesla died
Einstein died
Nietzsche died
Socrates died
Plato died
Aristotle died
King Henry XIII died
Death has no prejudice
Death is unconquerable
Even by the greatest conquerors in history
No one here gets out alive
Not even you

god?

If there is a god I wonder what he does in his spare time?
Also
Why do I think god is a he?
Is it
Society
Television
Education
Indoctrination
Parents
Newspapers
Books
Friends
Family
Uncles
Aunts
Grandparents
History
Biology
Prejudice
Because I'm a he?
Geography
Anthropology
Any ion or ogy
Is there one god
or many gods
With god jobs
A nine to five working god stiff
With their bitchy god wives
    "Honey you were supposed to build me a galaxy 6 billion year's ago and I'm still waiting"
With his god children screaming bloody hell
A masturbating
Depressed
Shitting
Drinking

Fucking
Hating
Lazy
Apathetic
Cowardly
Ugly
Suicidal god
Looking to take the easy way out
I could just see him now tying the rings of Saturn into a noose tight around his neck
Praying to his god for oblivion
Waiting for the black nothingness to creep towards everything
Sucked into a bag of empty space
The closest thing he'll ever come to death
Only to explode into another big bang
The sad realization of knowing he'll never die
The boredom of being all powerful
The meaninglessness
The infinite loneliness
I don't know
But if there is a god
I feel sorry for that son of a
?

The Smartest Man in the World

Take the smartest
Most brilliant
Philosophical
Mathematical genius
Everything savant
Space engineer
Nuclear physicist
Superman
Put him in a room with a
beautiful girl
and watch his intelligence
fade away

Sane Lunatics

Walking down
the streets of Dreg City
I see old government buildings
connected to each other
filled with lunatics who are sane
And sane lunatics
are the most normal
people in the world
Presidents, CEO's and Prime Ministers
all presented
as sane
everyday people
because they appear as
very civil and virtuous
pillars of the community
With their bowing heads, shaking hands,
smiles and good deeds done
Perfect citizens in public
But in private who wages war?
Who makes the decision
to send a plane full of explosives
to another country
to bomb the shit out of them?
    Your Government does
and who does the government buy their planes and bombs from?
    The Corporations
Who suffers?
    The People
Who profits?
    They do
Who allows it?
    The People
Now who's sane!
   and who's a lunatic?
You, Me, Them or All?

Modern Day Bukowski

Modern Day Bukowski
Minus the old time whores
introduce the willing and pretty
I sing and play rather than paint
the bank not the post office is my prison
Society still smells like shit and potpourri
The women aren't paid for with cash
but I wouldn't know'em if I didn't have it
and to get it
I have to sell my soul one hour at a time
Some may say my price is far more expensive then his
Not sure I agree
He was ugly as a teenager
I wasn't but I felt like it
I realized much later on
it wasn't me that was ugly
but society and its expectation of me
to finish high school
go to University, find a girl and job
get married, have kids
look like the people on TV
be a pillar of the community
Vote
at a mere cost of 40 hours a week
for the rest of my life
Sounds like a rip off job to me
Sounds like a sick crime
I should be prosecuted as a criminal
if I let this happen to myself
I'm sure he'd agree
maybe not
but If Bukowski read this poem
he'd roll over in his grave
puke and say
don't try

Space Invaders

I can't understand why people have so much trouble waiting!
Where do they have to go so quickly?
Two streetcars coming down the road
One in front of the other
The first streetcar is near full
The second near empty
Which streetcar do you think the people choose?
The first and the fullest
They pack in like animals going to the slaughter
Squishing together like human jello
Jiggling and coughing and spitting and talking
and puking and farting and body odour and eating and breathing and complaining and touching and spreading disease and reading the metro and listening to Ipods and talking on phones and on and on and on and on
For what?
The herd
They love it
Humans are herding animals
They actually like being around one another
 Lynching's and riots and wars and Nazi, Germany and The Crusades and The Inquisition and Slavery and making record profits off the starvation of entire continents with enough food to feed the world and watching the A-bomb explode
Why?
Because there's safety in numbers
You can hide in the herd
Act anonymously and with consent
Rape and murder and pillage and govern and profit and control all from the womb of the crowd
If everyone else is doing it, why can't I?
Logically it makes no sense and
perfect sense at the same time
That's what scares me about the world
This insane truth

Little Miracles (for Slayden)

I don't know what it feels like
to hold my own child
I don't know the look in their eyes
or the fears in their heart
I don't know the little miracles they perform everyday
The first scream
I'm sure is a miracle
The first smile
A miracle
The look on their face when they poop
A miracle
Hearing the words Daddy or Mommy
must be a miracle
The first steps
a miracle
Watching Parents be Grandparents
Brothers be Uncles or Fathers
Sisters be Aunties or Mothers
All little miracles
It seems to me most everything they do
might actually be miracles
and when I think about it
life is a miracle
If only more parents could treat their children like
the little miracles they are
This world might be a miraculous place to live
And when the time is right for me to have a child
it'll be a miracle
and I'll treat it as such

The Breath of Chance

When all you got left
is the hole in the bottom of your shoe
the wetness in your sock
the sadness in your heart
and the tears in your eyes
don't fret
there's more
You still have your breath
As long as you have breath
You still have a chance
And a chance is all you need

Don't Look in the Mirror

I had a dream
I was looking in the mirror
one of my teeth was loose
I was horrified
it was my vampire tooth on the left
I started touching it
it would wiggle more and more
I couldn't stop myself
I kept touching it
finally it came out and all I could think about was how much it was gonna cost to fix
I then started touching some of my other teeth
I noticed my gums were loose
all my teeth started falling out
Next thing you know I was toothless
I started pulling at the skin on my face
and it started coming off
chunk by chunk
like jello flesh
the whole time looking in the mirror
fascinated
I start pulling at my facial muscles
I left my eyes in so I could see everything
I pulled out my brain hoping to find my soul
but I found nothing
I woke up sweating

There's Drama in the Spiders Approach

Sitting their like an innocent vagrant
in some dirty corner of a dark room steeped in nothingness
The Spider waits in the abyss
only to come out to fix or feed
The Fly in its perfect wisdom
knows its role
and enjoys the shit it's living in
which is provided by all that dies
including yourself
Enjoys the same food as humans with no need of refrigeration
Racing through time a hundred miles an hour in any direction
Able to adapt to most anything
The epitome of evolution without the drama of human cooperation or
the lack there of
Looking for its next meal
Entrapped by the window pain
on the edge of its existence
Not understanding why it can't move any further
Thinking it found the end of the world
only to be trapped
by the invisible web of some unknown beast
Watching it stalk up the same invisible line
The Fly sensing the end is near
moves frantically
while the spider entombs it in a silk coffin
The Fly
feeling like its been had by some twisted game
dies alone with its very own Angel of Death
Much more terrifying then any human Angel of Death
The Spider waits
and waits
for its next meal

Sanely, Insane

Sanely, Insane
The strange thing is
It is the same
From one person to another
It will change
So what if you are a little deranged
Does your breath not come out the same place?
Those who claim to be sane strike me as vane
For the clock
is the god
they choose to praise
How can you measure infinite space?
Machines try but turn up blind
All the lights in the world
cannot take the suns shine
But humanity will not be denied
until they realize
the mistake of pride
While they march towards mass suicide
Their Pied Piper does not lie
He merely puts truth in disguise
And uses his talent to mesmerize
'Til one day
You end up on the other side
Where hate is faith
and false love has died
The only thing left is to come alive
And become everything you never tried
No more hatred
No more lies
Rise up
And become your life

The Most Beautiful Angel of All

An Angel of Light came to me in a dream
It was the most beautiful thing I'd ever seen
Its finger nails were black
and sparkly like the stars of night
I realized I wasn't talking to just any angel
but The Light Bringer himself
The Morning Star
The Fallen Son
The Most Beautiful Angel of All
I looked into his eyes and saw nothing
He stuck his tongue out
it was long and forked
he licked my face with it and began to talk
> You aren't like the rest
> You are perfect flesh
> Your soul has no meaning
> Your heart is empty
> and your mind is always seeking
> You are what all men should be
> You are my child
> and I your Father
> Let me hug you my precious boy

I was so terrified my eyes shook
> Do not be afraid my son
> I am here to help you
> Did I not help Eve in the Garden?
> Was it not I who guided her to the Tree of the Knowledge of Good and Evil?
> Was it not me who blessed man with the gift of intellect?
> Did I not show Adam he was naked?
> Who other then I gave man free will?
> Was it not I who released you from your cage of ignorance?

What would you be without me?
    An animal
What would this world be without me?
    A jungle

    I am the will behind the way
    I am the compass behind the truth
    I am the Angel of Men
    I am the Science of All Things
    I am the True Savior of Mankind
    What do you say to that my child?

You, like him are but a figment of my imagination
Mere words made into sentences made into stories
made into myths made into religion made into truth
You are no more real then Zeus, Apollo, Dionysius or Hades
You are an archetype used to control the minds of men
You are a goblin in a fairytale
At first I was afraid of you
But here in my dream I am the God you pretend to be
I am the power you speak of
You are none of what you say
You are no more then a thought in the mind of a man
    He began to shrink
    and fade
    I licked my thumb
    and index finger
    reached forward
    and put him out
    as if he were a candle

    Goodnight Father, he said

If

If I was on a safari I'd be a Lion
If I was a politician I'd be Machiavelli
If I was a leper I'd still be prettier then you
If I was to die now I'd know I lived
If I was a Poet I'd be Bukowski
If I was a commander I'd be Napoleon
If I was cancer I'd be Pancreatic
If I was a woman I'd be your mother
If I was an emotion I'd be anger
If I was a sin I'd be wrath
If I was lost you wouldn't find me
If I was a murderer you'd be dead
If I was a dream I'd be your worst nightmare
If I was a planet I'd be Jupiter
If I was God I'd start over
If I was an organ I'd be skin
If I was Jesus I wouldn't save you
If I was an A-Bomb I'd explode
If I was I a joke you wouldn't laugh
If everything was okay life wouldn't be worth it
If I was a bird I'd float
If I was the sun I'd burn
And if I was the devil
I'd be proud of humanity
If only things
were as easy
as if

The Order of Chaos

Is Order not Chaos itself?
Too much Order is Chaos
Too much Chaos is Order
If everything in the world
ran perfectly on time
all the time
Would that be perfect Order or perfect Chaos?
Is the chaos of the solar system on a deeper level actually a much larger form of Order?
Can orderly routines lead to disorder and madness?
Is genius
chaos disguised as madness
until the genius is able to
put its madness
into perfect order?
Einstein's theory of relativity
lead to the splitting of the atom
then the A-Bomb
chaos leads to order then order to chaos
Is this not the path all existence follows?
Is there such thing as perfect order or perfect chaos?
Spring, Summer
Fall, Winter
all happen every year in perfect order
We don't know exactly when they'll stop or start
or what kind of chaos each season will bring
but we do know they'll happen
Life is much the same way
Nothing would exist without Order and Chaos
It is the greatest gift the universe has to offer
Much like life and death
Order and Chaos are inexplicably connected
One cannot exist without the other
That's the beauty of it

Good, Evil or Will

People are so concerned with good or evil not realizing it's neither
it's simply the will of man
and the will of man does not concern itself with good or evil
It's not part of the equation
What will it take to conquer, is
Those few men who've championed morality
have been killed by those who don't
Jesus
Gandhi
Lennon
all dead
It seems the Nixon's, Stalin's and Mao's of the world are the ones who get to die from old age
Good and evil are meaningless words to these people
They understand do or don't
Death is a statistic
People aren't people
They're animals that come with the land
Just another resource on the human farm they call a country
Man needs to be controlled
like the cows
sheep
and chickens do
they are chattel
Do you ponder whether or not eating a cheese burger is good or evil?
No
and neither do men of power
How does the moral man take power from the immoral man, morally?
Every great nation is built on the crushed skulls
of a previous great nation, is it not?
Just ask the Natives in

Canada
The States
Australia
South Africa
Argentina
Mexico
or any land mass on this planet
Good and Evil wasn't pondered then
and it isn't pondered now
only the image of it
the reality is
it doesn't matter
only the will of man does

Time?

What is time?
    Is it not merely the division of a single moment into an infinite stream of small measurements?
What is it used for?
    To ensure people are on time for
        work?
            death?
                dinner?
                    taxes?
Is it not a method of enslavement?
    An invisible prison?
        The theft of life itself?
Is the clock not a sophisticated torture device used to steal the moment?
    Is it not an
        illusion?
            ghost?
                Mechanical God?
Does time have meaning?
  What does it mean for an hour
    to pass by
        For a day
            week or year
                to pass by?
Are people simply age?
    just a series of numbers?
        a collection of random information?
What would life be like without time?
    No early or late
      No punching in or out
      No schedule to follow
        No chaotic order to adhere to

Some people think time is a

    s
    t
    r
    a
    i
    g
    h
    t

    l
    i
    n
    e

With a beginning and an end
    Everything marching towards oblivion
        not realizing
            time is an ocean
and we are the whales swimming
    through
        its
          waves

We all die at the end

The comedy
oh,
the tragedy

Montreal (somebody's Dreg City but not mine)

Montreal

We came for the GSP fight
    but Montreal is not about GSP
It's not about the Canadians
  although I liked the Black Keys at the
      Bell Center
  It's not about the poutine
    although I do like the poutine
It's not about the old architecture
  although the cathedrals', cemeteries'
     gargoyles and temples are epic wonders
        of masonry
It's not about the beautiful women
  with their french accents and perfect bodies
    it's not about the amazing restaurants
      and great food
It's not about St. Catherine's and Crescent Street
    in the summertime
with the girls in tight
    dresses
        from all walks of life
          drunk, horny and ready to party
    No, it's not about that
It's not about the long stairways
    I'd be terrified to walk up or down
      if I was drunk
It's not about Chez Paree
    with their eye poppin french strippers
        in their little underwear no bigger
          then a four leaf clover
It's not about Grand Prix weekend
    or St. Patty's day
       drinking in the street
         watching the parade of women
           rather then the parade itself
    Who aren't afraid

        to drink and smoke
       to dance in the street
     to look like angels but act like demons
   Whose voices remind you of cobble streets,
old bicycles, picnics in the south of France
    and twirling frilly umbrella's
Oh Montreal
    The Paris of Canada
   Our own little piece of Europe
    Although it's not about that
       No,
      It's much more
Everywhere you go the people are happy
     You walk into a restaurant
         The hostess greets you
The manager says hello and makes jokes
      The waitress smiles and treats you proper
 You walk into a convenience store and the man
     jokes and laughs with you
Welcomes you to the city
  Even the guys you meet are cool
    Always suggesting great bars or clubs to visit
Even willing to take you to them
   The people of Montreal
     partying in the streets
enjoyin their lives in the cold as much as the heat
 They're a drug in themselves
    Oh Montreal how I want you
how I love you
  how I miss your arms around me
Oh Montreal we came for the fight
   but we found much more
     We found the soul of Montreal itself
       the people
         the beautiful people
              of 'Montreal, Montreal.......Montreal

Hotel Le Cantlie I apologize but I'm not sorry

Hotel Le Cantlie in Montreal
Canada's version of the Chateau Marmot
The room smells of cigarette and marijuana smoke
with a tinge of day old man
empty beer cans
decorate the place
like ornaments
on a horizontal Christmas tree
A small plate
full of cigarette butts and chicken bones
offends you
Remnants of food service lingers
half eaten
on the ground
Clothes everywhere
Liquor bottles
shine like little Eiffel towers
Tornados don't do as much damage as six
drunk men in a room
$25 tip on the table
Probably should have left $50
Upset security guards
Threats of eviction
Screaming
Falling over
Holes in the walls
and jokes
without limits
When you have a Chinese guy,
a White guy, a Jewish guy, A greasy Rock n Roller, a Brown guy
and a guy whose a mixture of all of the above
you can imagine
the kinds of jokes that were said
yet no one took offense
When you're friends

it doesn't matter what is said
All that matters is if it was funny
Did the boys laugh!
Especially on a road trip to Montreal
The place where angels come to die
and demons come to live
Hotel La Cantlie
I apologize
but I'm not sorry
See you next St. Patty's day

All Hail the King

I stumble into a bar
Wearing long greasy brown hair, a bowler hat and a green shirt that says "Stumble Inn"
St. Patty's day weekend in Montreal
I'm with a gang of Dregs
Rouge the Bear Jew
Rdog the Guyanese Indian
Chuman a third Chinese, a third white and a third something else
Barrett the photographer from Saskatchewan
Winston a full blown Chinese
and myself, Mitch the Rockstar
the gang of six
Winston finds a Burger King crown
Puts it on
with a slight right angle tilt like Jughead
from the Archie comics
He has caramel skin and a round face
It seems serendipity has selected our King for us
I start screaming
    Make way for the King
    All hail the King
    Make way for the King
Much like a herald proclaims the King
    Make way for the King
    All hail the King
He even waves like a King
A slightly cupped right hand
looking side to side
a gentle tilt to his head
a very regal look on his face
The people
confused
nervously step back
It dawns on me
They're actually making way for the King

Two people come by, bow and say
    Sire
Next thing you know we're all yelling
    Make way for the king
    All hail the King
The people start hootin and hollering
The waitress asks for the King's name
    King Winston the First he says
    May I kiss your hand my Liege?
    You may
The King motions to a girl
points at one of his minions
    GIVE HIM SOME HEAD he yells
To laughter and applause
A man comes up and says
    You don't look like a King
    But your friend looks like Kid Rock
The King looks at his disciples and screams in
a high pitched whiney voice
  with an emphasis on the long E
  in a Kid Rock kind of way
    My Name is Keeeeiiinngg!!!!
The boys erupt
    Fall over with laughter
We all start mimicking him in unison
    My Name is Keeeeiiinng!!!
The world is grooving to our beat
At this moment we are six people
experiencing the exact same feeling
at the exact same time
perfect synchronicity is contagious
the people around us are swallowed up by our energy
The owner, the patrons, the waitresses
all want a piece of the King and his Dregs
We order a round of Tequila shots
with Tabasco sauce
and everyone screams at the same time

      TO THE KING!!!
We decide it's time to leave
I bellow
      Stop everyone the King speaks
Everyone in the bar freezes
and stare at the King
like a car accident
The King pauses slightly, looks around at the bar patrons and says
      "So long……suckers"
He gives a kingly twirl with his right hand
and walks out the door
the crowd explodes in laughter
good cheer drippin off the walls
The waitress's mouth is wide open
foaming like a mad dog
The Kings crew
keels over
holding onto their guts
for dear life
The crowd
with their bulging eyes
and big yellow teeth
not unlike
characters
from the Black Hole Sun video
rabidly applaud their new King
The rest of us hit the street like clowns out of a small car
We stumble on to our next adventure
All hail the King

Alice

I met a girl in Montreal from Paris
Dirty blonde curly brown hair
Much like the classic French girl
I'm with my buddy Winston
at McKibbons on St. Laurent
Packed house
A band called "The Jones"
is playin
I ask if she wants a drink
    I'll have an orange juice
I ignore the order
Her friend comes up
Very physically unattractive
a big nose
small chin
brown hair
might be a full out lesbian
looks like a female Joey Ramone
but uglier
I take my jacket off
I'm wearing a T-shirt
with an image of
Charles Bukowski
sitting on a park bench
wearing a toque
with his name at the
bottom of the picture
They both notice it at the same time
    "Oh you like Bukowksi?"
    -"Ya he's my favorite writer"-
They whisper to each other
and introduce themselves
    "I'm Alice" says the girl I like
The other one says her name
I can't understand nor care to hear it

-"Do you girls want a drink?"-
"Ya I'll have a Rum and Orange juice" says Alice
Strange order I think to myself
but easy to remember
The other one orders a drink to
but I don't recall what it was
Other then her grotesque appearance
Nothing she did
struck me as memorable
or interesting
She was more of an obstacle
or a red light
an object in the background
of the life of Alice than anything else
She's so terrible looking my buddy
couldn't even play wing man
The band is crushing
great tune after great tune
"When I come around" by Greenday
"Whole Lotta Love" by Zep
"About a girl" by Nirvana
Alice and I are grooving
Mimicking each others steps
She moves like a gazelle
I feel like a lion
she has little mole on her lip
like Cindy Crawford
her eyes brown and sophisticated
enchant me
We dance
as if we are alone
even though we're surrounded by people
She takes my bowler hat off
starts wearing it
Everything she does is sexy
All of a sudden
we hear the intro to

"Killing in the Name of" by Rage
    bump, bump, badadaadada
    bump, bump, bdadadadada
    bump, bump, badadaadada
    bump, bump, bdadadadada
We end up at the front of the stage
So close we can feel the bands breath
The vultures start to swarm
as a pit forms
She's grinding her ass on my piece
I have my arms around her
Protecting her from the non alpha-males
And the song kicks in
    "Killing the name of"
People jumping up and down
Moshing around
I push back and block out
a small spot for Alice
my aim is to protect and grind her
She's rocking and digging the music
A gazelle in a pit of lions
I
transfixed
in the moment
enjoy my role
Throw a couple elbows
and hard looks at people
to let them know I mean business
they back off
understanding the hierarchy
The world is full of animals
and if you don't act like one
from time to time
you'll lose
the song grinds to a whisper and
slowly builds
    Fuck you I won't do what you tell me

The energy in the room is explosive
The beat takes us away to our youth
    Fuck you I won't do what you tell me
Where the only worries you had
was what album you were gonna buy
or does this girl like me
    Fuck you I won't do what you tell me
Everything else meant nothing
The world was so innocent
and simple
Music was life itself
    Fuck you I won't do what you tell me
The crowd starts screaming in unison
    Fuck you I won't do what you tell me
The crowd bounces off each other
like fleshy pin balls, screamin
    Fuck you I won't do what you tell me
people start randomly hugging
and cheersing
as the music pumps in the background
this is what life's about
letting go of inhibitions
of other peoples thoughts
and expectations of yourself
just flowing unabashedly
with the moment
in celebration of your fellow man
with your fellow man
if only the music could last forever
humanity might get somewhere
the song finishes
the crowd applauds
Alice and I both gassed
leave the dance floor
She kisses me on the cheek
Thanks me
and leaves

I'll probably never see her again
doesn't matter
it's not about the future
you have with someone
but the time spent
it's not about sex
it's about experience
It seems some of the best times
I've ever had with girls
didn't include sex
Cheers to all the girls out there
who have unknowingly
changed my life
by just being yourself

Jewish Jersey Girl in Montreal

I met a Jersey girl in Montreal
Jewish with a heart as golden as her hair
who needs to keep her marks up
so she can become an FBI agent
She's with a friend that looks like a sad oven mitt
who doesn't like me
cuz she thinks I'm slimy and prefers guys
that actually shower
I'm sure she also likes long walks on the beach,
eating cornflakes
and getting dry humped by guys named
Bruce or Thaddeus
I ignore her
and continue to chat
with my Jersey girl
She tells me both her parents
are self made millionaires
and that she plans on makin
her own way in this life
Her smile reminds me of California
but she's from the Jersey Shore
She's only slept with 2 guys in her whole life
both were assholes
Apparently she's attracted to them
that explains why she's talkin to me
I pull her chair close
put my arm around her
and we continue to talk
My friends want to go to the next bar
But I refuse
I'm havin too good a time
with my beautiful Jewish girl from Jersey
She tells me her best friend in high school
made her life hell
Spread rumors

Told her she was ugly
and ruined her self esteem
She also told me her best friend had herpes
Now there's a rumor
While she's talking to me I rub her back
She's wearing black tights
I run my fingers down the top of them
I can feel her thong through the back
They're lacey
I let my fingers follow the lines of the v
to their natural conclusion
her ass
I grab it
She looks at me with comfort in her eyes
Sometimes just feelin
a girl's ass
who's pouring her heart out to you
is the best thing in the world
I could stay with her all day
all night
all week
all month
all year
just listen to her
and rub her back
I get her phone number
cuz I gotta leave
I text her
She promises to get back to me
I'm still waiting
Bianca if you ever read this poem
know
I still think about you from time to time
and if you ever do become an FBI agent
please don't arrest me

Acknowledgements

I would like to thank Greg Simon for taking the cover photo of this book. The photo is a story in itself which will be written one day.

Matt Ross

Contact Information

Matt Ross
Kingofthedregs@live.com
Like me on Facebook at www.facebook.com/dregcity

Made in the USA
Middletown, DE
27 May 2019